I0822105

BUFFALO BILLS

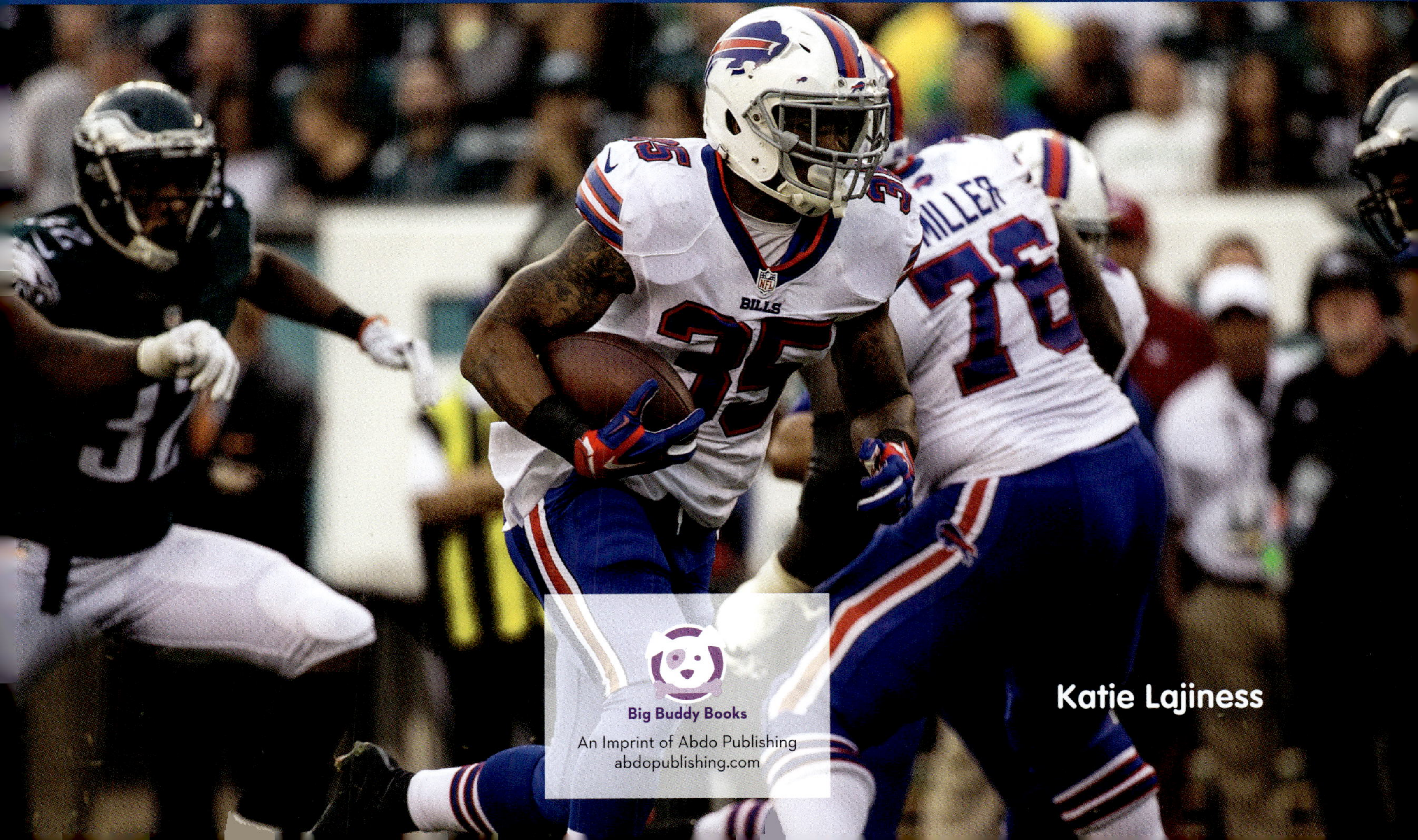

Katie Lajiness

Big Buddy Books
An Imprint of Abdo Publishing
abdopublishing.com

abdopublishing.com

Published by Abdo Publishing, a division of ABDO, PO Box 398166, Minneapolis, Minnesota 55439.

Printed in the United States of America, North Mankato, Minnesota.
092016
012017

Cover Photo: ASSOCIATED PRESS.
Interior Photos: ASSOCIATED PRESS.

Coordinating Series Editor: Tamara L. Britton
Graphic Design: Michelle Labatt, Taylor Higgins, Jenny Christensen

Publisher's Cataloging-in-Publication Data

Names: Lajiness, Katie, author.
Title: Buffalo Bills / by Katie Lajiness.
Description: Minneapolis, MN : Abdo Publishing, 2017. | Series: NFL's greatest teams | Includes bibliographical references and index.
Identifiers: LCCN 2016944873 | ISBN 9781680785296 (lib. bdg.) | ISBN 9781680798890 (ebook)
Subjects: LCSH: Buffalo Bills (Football team)--History--Juvenile literature.
Classification: DDC 796.332--dc23
LC record available at http://lccn.loc.gov/2016944873

Contents

A Winning Team

The Buffalo Bills are a football team from Buffalo, New York. They have played in the National Football League (NFL) for almost 60 years.

The Bills have had good seasons and bad. But time and again, they've proven themselves. Let's see what makes the Bills one of the NFL's greatest teams.

Blue, red, and white are the team's colors.

Lite
OFFICIAL BEER SPONSOR OF THE
OFFICIAL BEER SPONSOR

League Play

Team Standings

The AFC and the National Football Conference (NFC) make up the NFL. Each conference has a north, south, east, and west division.

The NFL got its start in 1920. Its teams have changed over the years. Today, there are 32 teams. They make up two conferences and eight divisions.

The Bills play in the East Division of the American Football Conference (AFC). This division also includes the Miami Dolphins, the New England Patriots, and the New York Jets.

Fans get excited to watch the Bills play!

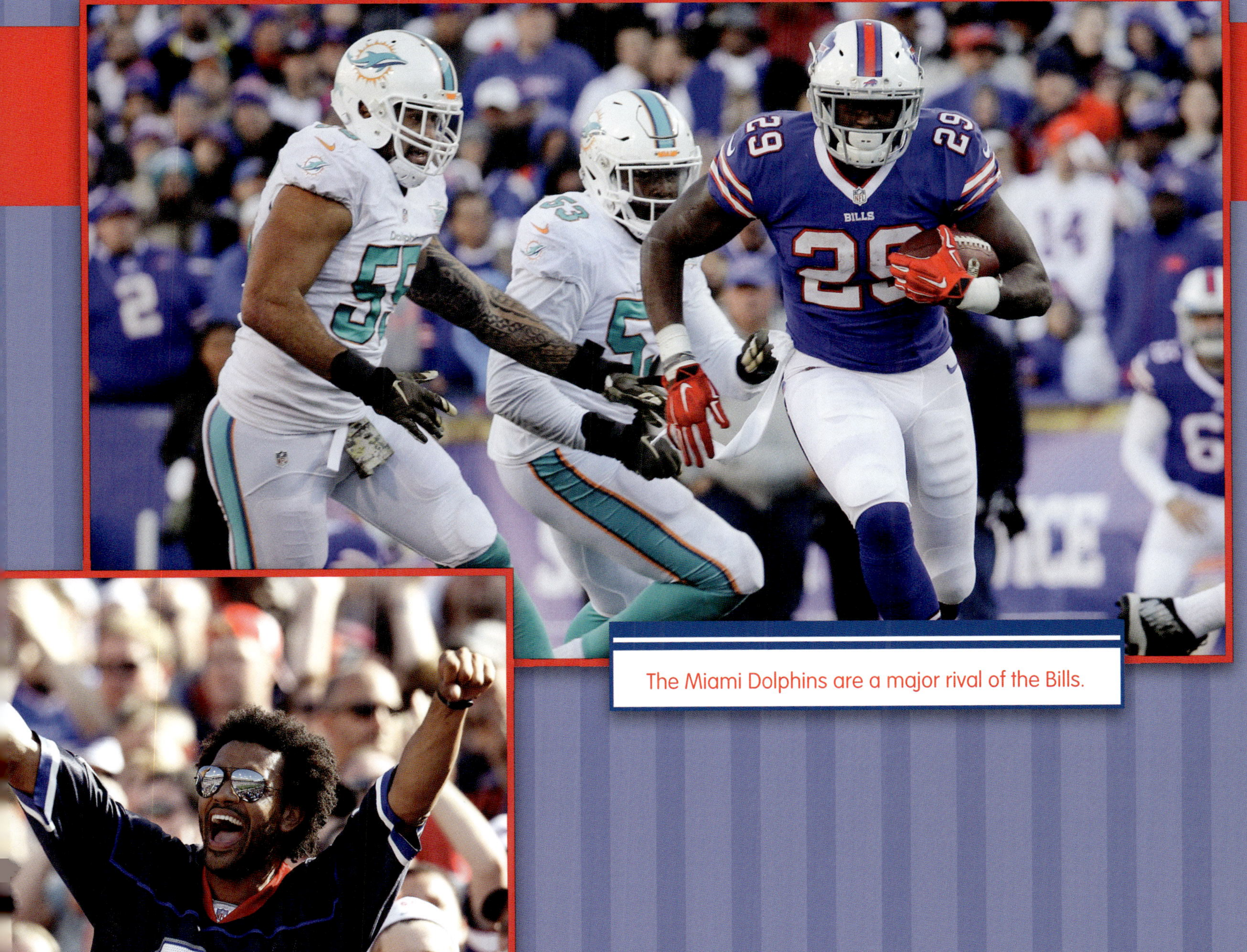

The Miami Dolphins are a major rival of the Bills.

Kicking Off

Businessman Ralph C. Wilson Jr. founded the Buffalo Bills in 1959. The team played its first game the next year. They were one of eight teams in the American Football League (AFL).

In 1963, the Bills tied with the Boston Patriots for the best record in the AFL Eastern Division. So, the two teams played a tie-breaker game. The Bills lost 26–8.

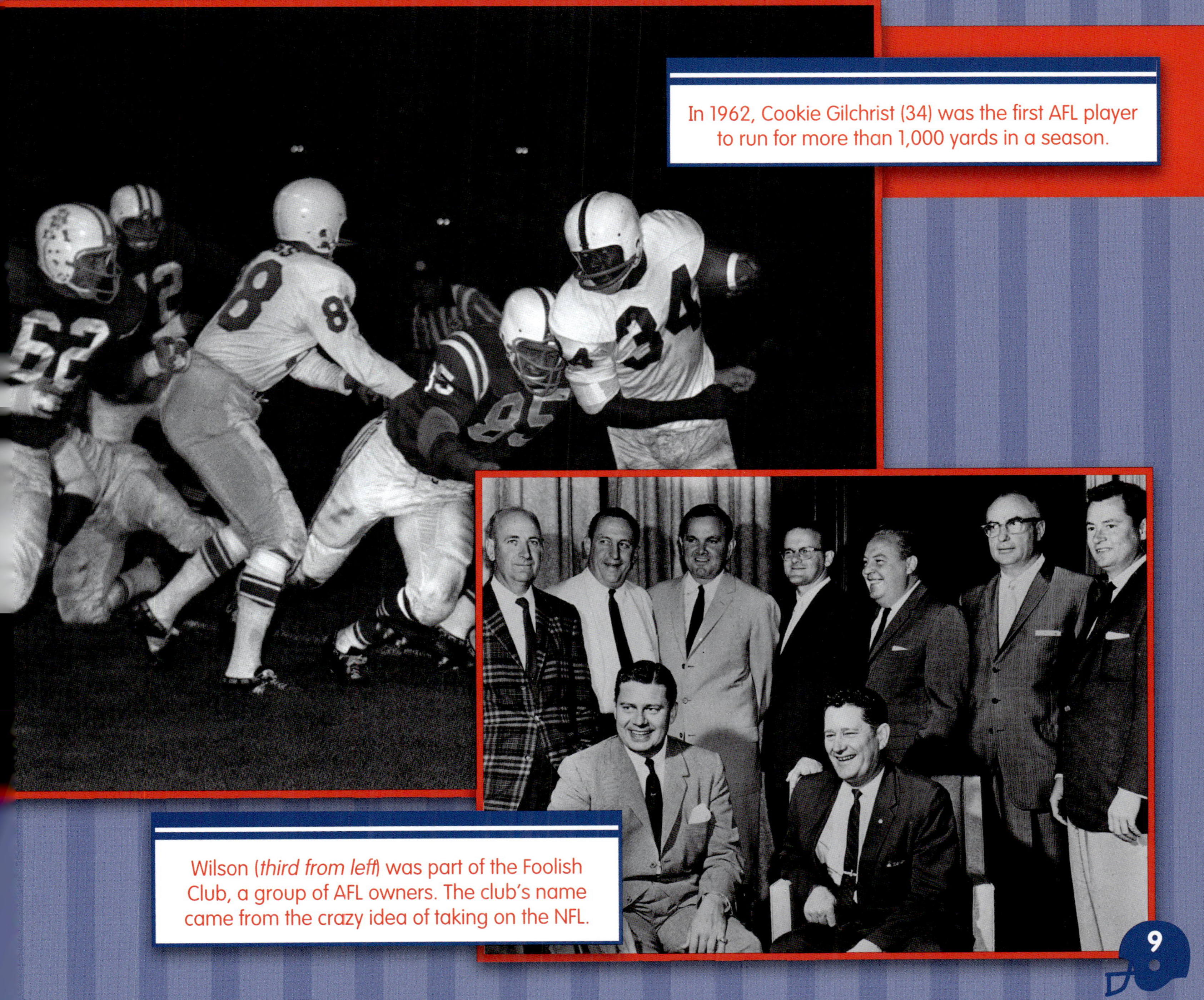

In 1962, Cookie Gilchrist (34) was the first AFL player to run for more than 1,000 yards in a season.

Wilson (*third from left*) was part of the Foolish Club, a group of AFL owners. The club's name came from the crazy idea of taking on the NFL.

Highlight Reel

Win or Go Home

NFL teams play 16 regular season games each year. The teams with the best records are part of the play-off games. Play-off winners move on to the conference championships. Then, conference winners face off in the Super Bowl!

In 1964 and 1965, the Bills won their division. Then, they played in the AFL **championship**. The Bills beat the San Diego Chargers both times to become champions!

The next year, the team made it to the AFL championship again. But, this time they lost to the Kansas City Chiefs. With this loss, the Bills missed playing in the first Super Bowl.

Coach Lou Saban (*left*) led the Bills to AFL championships in 1964 and 1965.

In 1964, the Bills played at Shea Stadium. This was the home stadium of the New York Jets. The Bills upset the Jets in front of a crowd of 61,000.

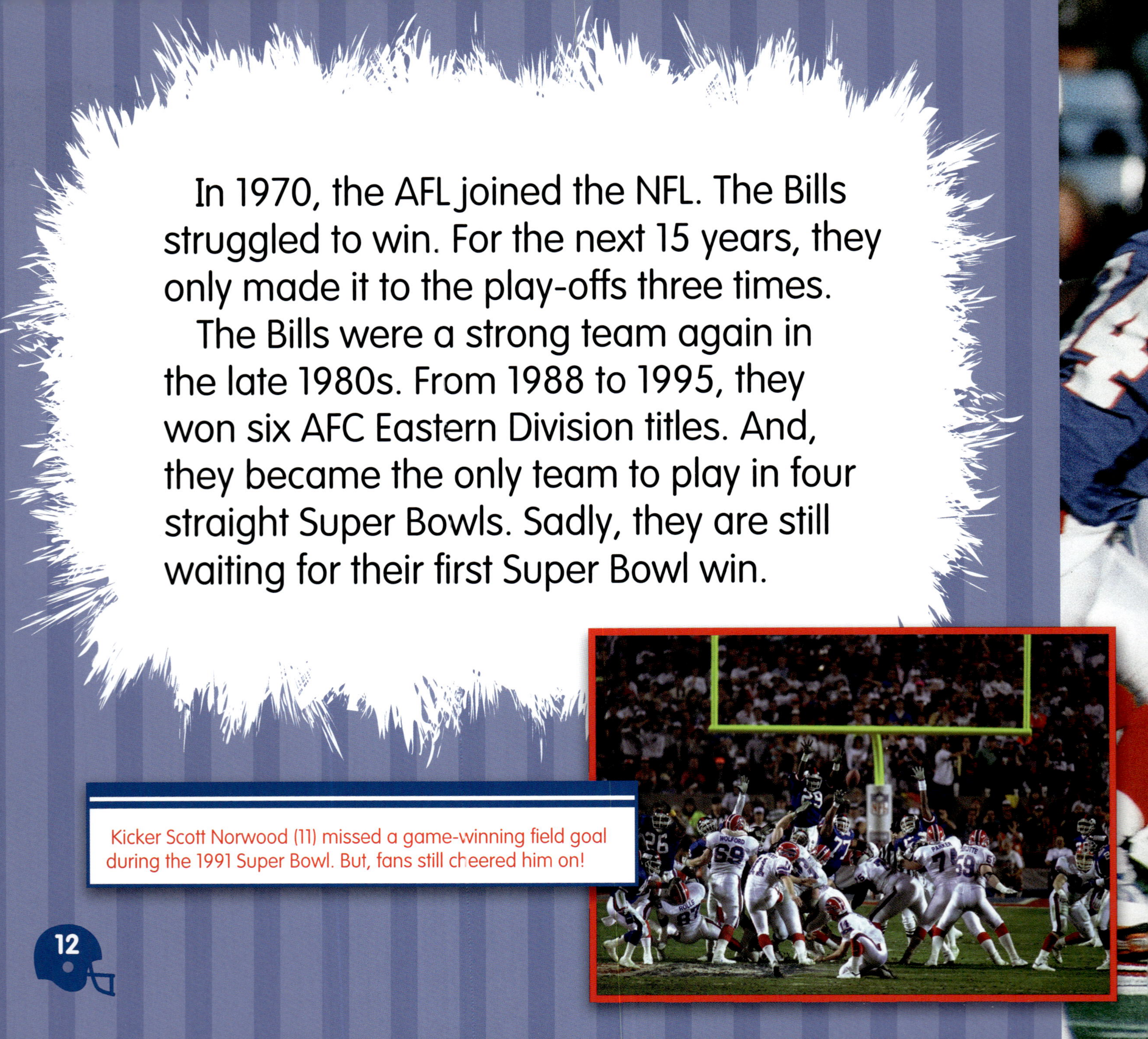

In 1970, the AFL joined the NFL. The Bills struggled to win. For the next 15 years, they only made it to the play-offs three times.

The Bills were a strong team again in the late 1980s. From 1988 to 1995, they won six AFC Eastern Division titles. And, they became the only team to play in four straight Super Bowls. Sadly, they are still waiting for their first Super Bowl win.

Kicker Scott Norwood (11) missed a game-winning field goal during the 1991 Super Bowl. But, fans still cheered him on!

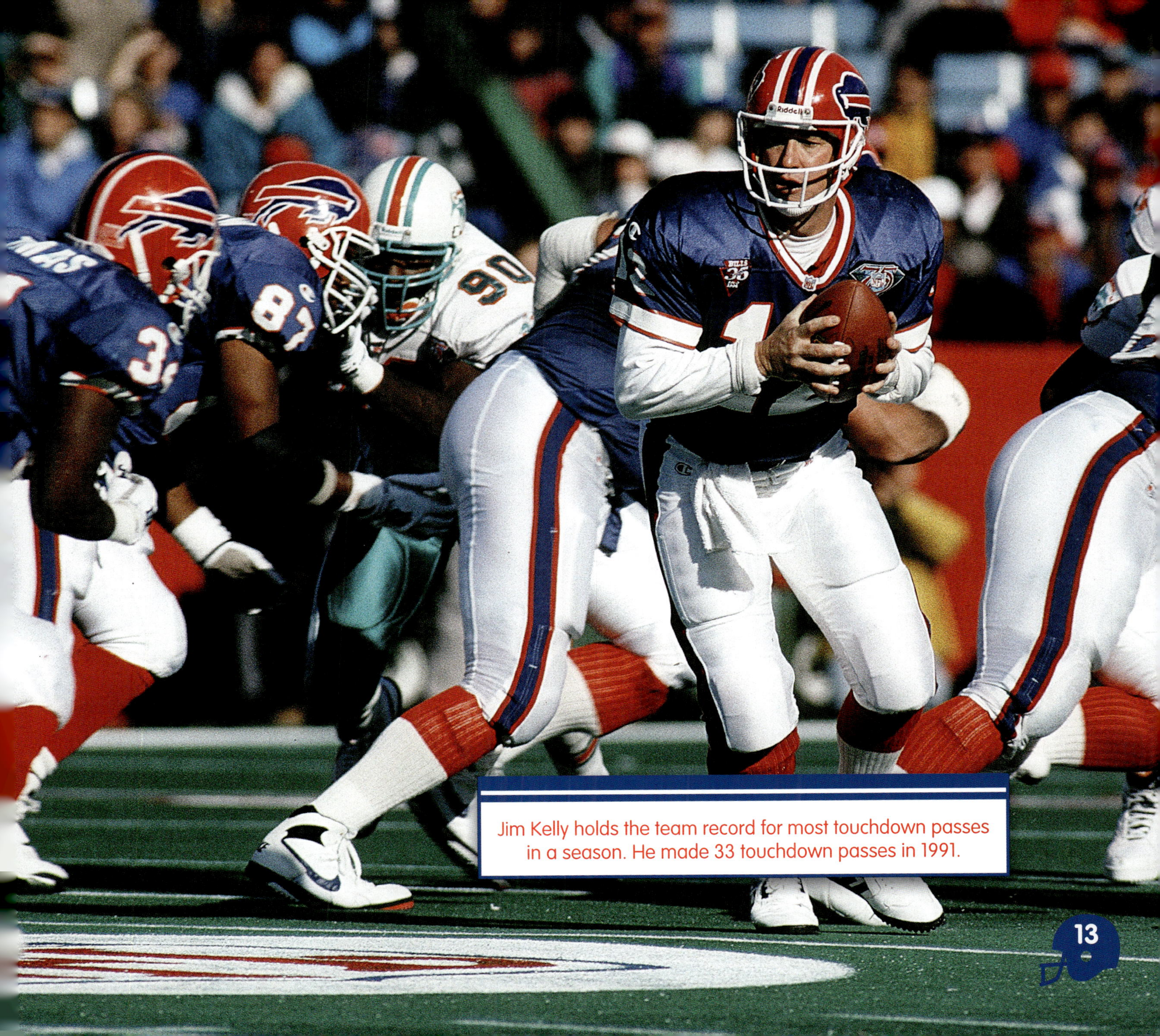

Jim Kelly holds the team record for most touchdown passes in a season. He made 33 touchdown passes in 1991.

Halftime! Stat Break

Team Records

RUSHING YARDS
Career: Thurman Thomas, 11,938 yards (1988–1999)
Single Season: O.J. Simpson, 2,003 yards (1973)

PASSING YARDS
Career: Jim Kelly, 35,467 yards (1986–1996)
Single Season: Drew Bledsoe, 4,359 yards (2002)

RECEPTIONS
Career: Andre Reed, 941 receptions (1985–1999)
Single Season: Eric Moulds, 100 receptions (2002)

ALL-TIME LEADING SCORER
Norm Johnson, 810 points, (1982–1990)

Championships

EARLY CHAMPIONSHIP WINS:
1964, 1965

SUPER BOWL APPEARANCES:
1991, 1992, 1993, 1994

SUPER BOWL WINS:
None

Famous Coaches

Lou Saban (1962–1965, 1972–1976)
Chuck Knox (1978-1982)
Marv Levy (1986–1997)

Pro Football Hall of Famers & Their Years with the Bills

Joe DeLamielleure, Guard (1973–1979, 1985)
Jim Kelly, Quarterback (1986–1996)
Marv Levy, Coach (1986–1997)
Bill Polian, Contributor (1984–1992)
Andre Reed, Wide Receiver (1985–1999)
Billy Shaw, Guard (1961–1969)
O.J. Simpson, Running Back (1969–1977)
Bruce Smith, Defensive End (1985–1999)
Thurman Thomas, Running Back (1988–1999)
Ralph C. Wilson Jr., Founder/Owner (1960–2014)

Fan Fun

STADIUM: Ralph Wilson Stadium
LOCATION: Orchard Park, New York
MASCOT: Billy Buffalo
TEAM SONG: "Shout"

Coaches' Corner

Chuck Knox led the Bills to an AFC Eastern Division title in 1980. That year, he was named NFL Coach of the Year. Knox coached many talented Bills players. Some of them won NFL Player of the Year **awards**.

Marv Levy became head coach of the Bills in 1986. He quickly turned the Bills into a winning team. Under Levy, the team had eight winning seasons. And, they went to the Super Bowl four times.

Levy was the oldest coach in the NFL when he coached his last season in 1997. He was 72.

Knox coached the team from 1978 to 1982.

In 2015, Rex Ryan became the team's new head coach.

Star Players

O.J. Simpson RUNNING BACK (1969–1977)

In 1972, O.J. Simpson led the league in rushing yards. The next year, he became the first player to rush for more than 2,000 yards in a season! Simpson was also named NFL Most Valuable Player (MVP). He joined the Pro Football Hall of Fame in 1985.

Joe DeLamielleure GUARD (1973–1979, 1985)

The Bills chose Joe DeLamielleure in the first round of the 1973 **draft**. He was part of the team's powerful offensive line. In 1975, DeLamielleure was named Offensive Lineman of the Year. He was selected to play in six Pro Bowls, which is the NFL's all-star game.

Andre Reed WIDE RECEIVER (1985–1999)

Andre Reed was a key player during the team's glory years. He was known for his ability to rush after catching a pass. Reed is the team's all-time leading receiver with 941 receptions for 13,095 yards. He also has 87 **career** touchdowns with the Bills. Reed is tied for most with teammate Thurman Thomas.

Bruce Smith DEFENSIVE END (1985–1999)

Bruce Smith was the team's first pick in the 1985 **draft**. During his 15-year **career** with the Bills, he recorded 171 sacks. That is a team record! Smith was named the NFL Defensive Player of the Year in 1990 and 1996. And, he was invited to play in the Pro Bowl 11 times.

Jim Kelly QUARTERBACK (1986–1996)

Jim Kelly was known for making quick decisions in a fast-paced offense. During his career, he threw 237 touchdowns. Kelly helped the team get to four Super Bowls! In 2002, he became a member of the Pro Football Hall of Fame.

Thurman Thomas RUNNING BACK (1988–1999)

Thurman Thomas rushed for more than 1,000 yards in eight straight seasons with the Bills. Only four other players have done that in NFL history! Thomas was named NFL MVP in 1991 and Offensive Player of the Year in 1992.

Tyrod Taylor QUARTERBACK (2015–)

Tyrod Taylor became the starting quarterback in 2015. In his first **career** NFL start, he earned a win by beating the Indianapolis Colts 27–14. That season, Taylor set a quarterback team record for rushing. In 2016, he played in his first Pro Bowl.

Ralph Wilson Stadium

The Bills play home games at Ralph Wilson Stadium. It is in Orchard Park, New York. Ralph Wilson Stadium opened in 1973. It holds about 73,000 people.

The Bills are the only NFL team that plays its home games in New York State. The New York Jets and The New York Giants play in New Jersey.

pepsi
TOYOTA
BILLS

Go Bills!

Thousands of fans flock to Ralph Wilson Stadium to see the Bills play home games.

In 2000, the team got a **mascot**. Billy Buffalo wears a jersey with the letters BB. He appears at home games to help fans cheer on their team.

Bills fans will brave the cold and snow to watch their favorite team.

Final Call

The Bills have a long, rich history. They appeared in four straight Super Bowls!

Even during losing seasons, true fans have stuck by them. Many believe the Buffalo Bills will remain one of the greatest teams in the NFL.

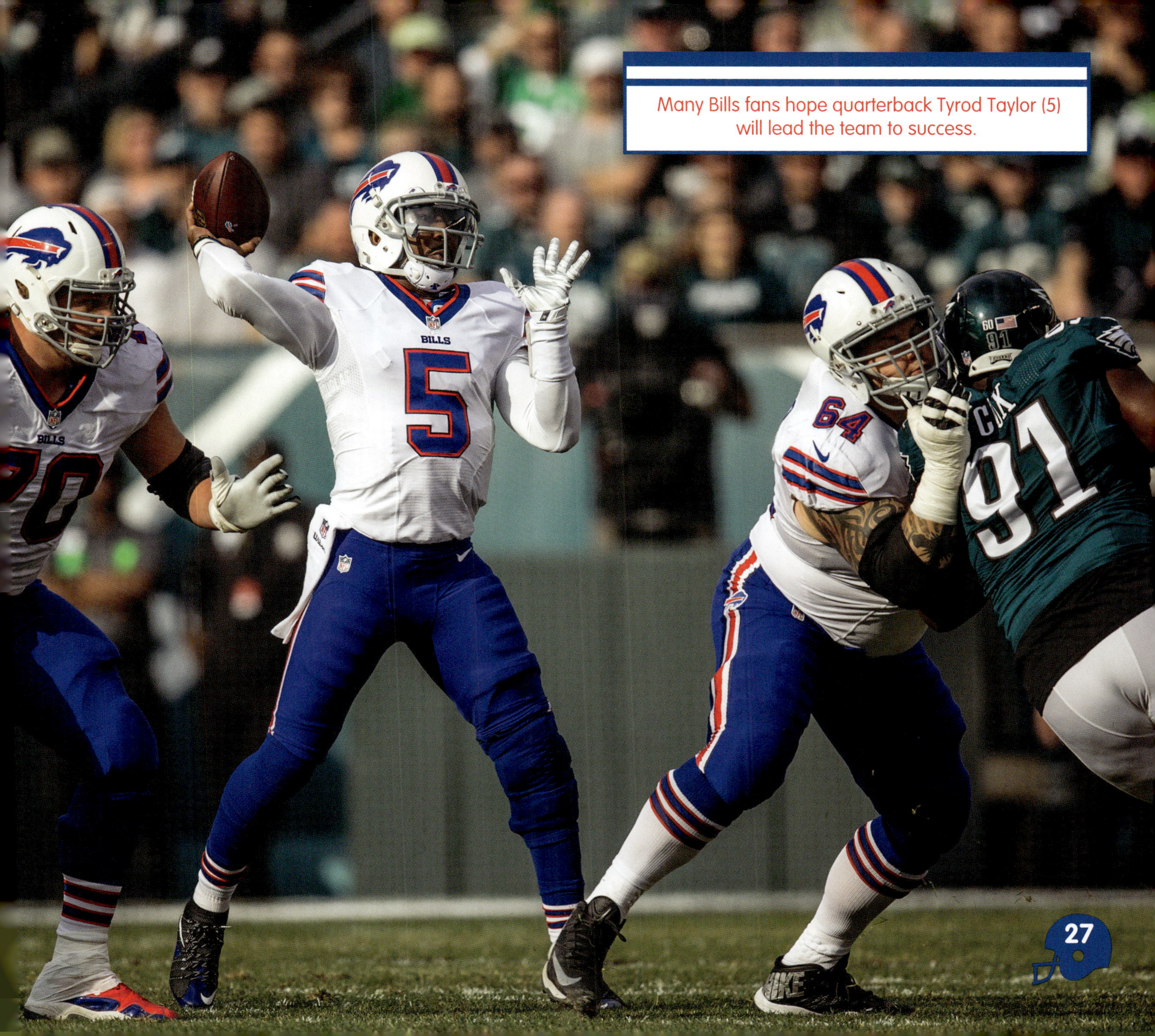

Many Bills fans hope quarterback Tyrod Taylor (5) will lead the team to success.

Through the Years

1960

The Buffalo Bills play their first season in the AFL.

1964–1965

The Bills win two straight AFL **championships**!

1970

The AFL joins the NFL.

1975

O.J. Simpson sets an NFL record when he scores 23 touchdowns during the season.

1988

Marv Levy is named NFL Coach of the Year.

1991–1994

The Bills play in four straight Super Bowls! This is an NFL record.

1998

The team's stadium is renamed Ralph Wilson Stadium.

2014

Businessman Terry Pegula is the new owner of the Buffalo Bills.

2015

The Bills introduce new uniforms.

Postgame Recap

1. What is the mascot for the Bills?
   A. Baboon **B**. Bison **C**. Buffalo

2. How may Super Bowls have the Bills played in?
   A. 3
   B. 4
   C. 5

3. What is the name of the stadium where the Bills play home games?
   A. Ralph Wilson Stadium
   B. Jim Kelly Stadium
   C. Buffalo Bills Stadium

4. Name three 3 of the 10 Bills in the Pro Football Hall of Fame.

1. C. 2. B. 3. A 4. See page 15

Glossary

award something that is given in recognition of good work or a good act.

career a period of time spent in a certain job.

champion the winner of a championship, which is a game, a match, or a race held to find a first-place winner.

draft a system for professional sports teams to choose new players.

mascot something to bring good luck and help cheer on a team.

Websites

To learn more about the NFL's Greatest Teams, visit **booklinks.abdopublishing.com**. These links are routinely monitored and updated to provide the most current information available.

Index